HISTORY'S MOST INFLUENTIAL WRITERS

FROM THE 700s BCE TO THE 1500s

Homer to Edmund Spenser

EDITED BY J.E. LUEBERING

Britannica® Educational Publishing

IN ASSOCIATION WITH

ROSEN EDUCATIONAL SERVICES

Published in 2025 by Britannica Educational Publishing
(a trademark of Encyclopædia Britannica, Inc.)
in association with Rosen Educational Services, LLC
2544 Clinton Street, Buffalo, NY 14224.

Distributed exclusively by Rosen Educational Services.
For a listing of additional Britannica Educational Publishing titles, call toll free (800) 237-9932.

First Edition

Britannica Educational Publishing
Michael I. Levy: Executive Editor
Marilyn L. Barton: Senior Coordinator, Production Control
Steven Bosco: Director, Editorial Technologies
Lisa S. Braucher: Senior Producer and Data Editor
Yvette Charboneau: Senior Copy Editor
Kathy Nakamura: Manager, Media Acquisition
J. E. Luebering: Manager and Senior Editor, Literature

Editor: Greg Roza
Book design: Michael Flynn

Photo credits: Cover Timothy Harding/Shutterstock.com; p. 11 Vasileios Karafillidis/Shutterstock.com; p. 25 https://commons.wikimedia.org/wiki/File:Virgil_Chaudet_Cour_Carr%C3%A9e_Louvre.jpg; p. 41 Kotroz/Shutterstock.com; p. 55 Portrait of Michel de Montaigne, circa unknown.jpg

Cataloging-in-Publication Data

Names: Luebering, J.E.
Title: From the 700s BCE to the 1500s: Homer to Edmund Spenser / edited by J.E. Luebering.
Description: New York : Britannica Educational Publishing, in Association with Rosen Educational Services, 2025. | Series: History's most influential writers | Includes glossary and index.
Identifiers: ISBN 9781641901055 (library bound) | ISBN 9781641901048 (pbk) | ISBN 9781641901062 (ebook)
Subjects: LCSH: Authors, Classical--Biography. | Classical literature--History and criticism. | Literature, Ancient--History and criticism. | Authorship--History--To 1500.
Classification: LCC PN621.F766 2025 | DDC 880.09 B--dc23

Manufactured in the United States of America

CPSIA Compliance Information: Batch #CSBRIT25. For further information contact Rosen Publishing at 1-800-237-9932.

Find us on

CONTENTS

Introduction

"I write to keep from going mad from the contradictions I find among mankind—and to work some of those contradictions out for myself."
—Michel de Montaigne (1533–1592)

Open a book—any book. In it you'll find words, of course, but look closely and you'll also find art, crafted, in detail, by a writer proud enough to sign his or her name to the work. In a book, or in any piece of writing, words are joined together at the whim of the author. Sentences are created, paragraphs and stanzas formatted, chapters built, and stories told. In a book or a poem, a play or a short story, everything is there, on the page, for a reason: To show, to tell, to convey a message. Most works of writing, quite simply, are meant for reading. The great ones, however, by the most talented and ingenious authors, are for study. In such works, it's the art one finds within that sets them apart from the rest.

Writers are influenced by the places in which they live and the cultures in which they are steeped. The writers in this volume are all "greats" who lived between the 7th century BCE and the 16th century CE. Several individuals included in this compilation, such as Geoffrey Chaucer, are paradigms of English literature. Others, such as Sophocles, Aeschylus, and Aristophanes, hail from ancient Greece. The 13th-century Sufi poet Rūmī is known today as a musically influenced master on subjects like mysticism, love, and spirituality.

As the title of this book indicates, all those featured in this collection are influential writers. Through their work, they reached out to the masses, touched the hearts and souls of millions, and left their mark on the world. But how exactly is influence defined in this case? Perhaps it's the ability of one person, through his or her writing, to change the way the world thinks.

Perhaps a writer's influence is determined by timeless prominence, the ability to remain relevant hundreds of years after initial publication. All of the authors in this book fit that bill. This ability to sway audiences so deeply, and in so many ways, several centuries after the fact is arguably the very definition of influential.

With carefully crafted prose or a verse, a writer can influence individual allegiances, support or defame a political regime, or effect change by shedding light on an untenable situation. When all is said and done, perhaps what makes a writer influential is simply the ability to entertain, to keep readers up at night, turning page after page, just so they can learn what happens next.

The truth is, influence can mean so many things and can be measured in so many ways. Those who read the works of any of the writers profiled in this book may very well discover an experience they've perhaps never had before. They might have their imagination sparked and be transported, however briefly, from the travails of the life they're living. An author's writing might, with its insight, highlight an injustice, leading readers to speak out themselves and demand an equitable resolution. Whatever the case, one can't read a work by authors such as those detailed here without being influenced in some way. That's the power of great writing. And that's the real reason we read.

HOMER

(flourished 9th or 8th century BCE?, Ionia? [now in Turkey])

Homer is the presumed author of the *Iliad* and the *Odyssey*. Although these two great epic poems of ancient Greece have always been attributed to the shadowy figure of Homer, little is known of him beyond the fact that his was the name attached in antiquity by the Greeks themselves to the poems. That there was an epic poet called Homer and that he played the primary part in shaping the *Iliad* and the *Odyssey*—so much may be said to be probable. If this assumption is accepted, then Homer must assuredly be one of the greatest of the world's literary artists.

He is also one of the most influential authors in the widest sense, for the two epics provided the basis of Greek education and culture throughout the Classical age and formed the backbone of humane education down to the time of the Roman Empire and the spread of Christianity. Indirectly through the medium of Virgil's *Aeneid* (loosely molded after the patterns of the *Iliad* and the *Odyssey*), directly through their revival under Byzantine culture from the late 8th century CE onward, and subsequently through their passage into Italy with the Greek scholars who fled westward from the Ottomans, the Homeric epics had a profound impact on the Renaissance culture of Italy. Since then the proliferation of translations has helped to make them the most important poems of the classical European tradition.

Early References

Implicit references to Homer and quotations from the poems date to the middle of the 7th century BCE. Archilochus, Alcman, Tyrtaeus, and Callinus in the 7th century and Sappho and others in the early 6th adapted Homeric phraseology and meter to their own purposes and rhythms. At the same time scenes from the epics became popular in works of art. The pseudo-Homeric "Hymn to Apollo of Delos," probably of late 7th-century composition, claimed to be the work of "a blind man who dwells in rugged Chios," a reference to a tradition about Homer himself. The idea that Homer had descendants known as "Homeridae," and that they had taken over the preservation and propagation of his poetry, goes back at least to the early 6th century BCE.

It was not long before a kind of Homeric scholarship began: Theagenes of Rhegium in southern Italy toward the end of the same century wrote the first of many allegorizing interpretations. By the 5th century biographical fictions were well under way. The Pre-Socratic philosopher Heracleitus of Ephesus made use of a trivial legend of Homer's death—that it was caused by chagrin at not being able to solve some boys' riddle about catching lice—and the concept of a contest of quotations between Homer and Hesiod (after Homer, the most ancient of Greek poets) may have been initiated in the Sophistic tradition. The historian Herodotus assigned the formulation of Greek theology to Homer and Hesiod, and claimed that they could have lived no more than 400 years before his own time, the 5th century BCE. This should be contrasted with the superficial assumption, popular in many circles throughout antiquity, that Homer must have lived not much later than the Trojan War about which he sang.

The general belief that Homer was a native of Ionia (the central part of the western seaboard of Asia Minor) seems a reasonable conjecture for the poems themselves are in predominantly Ionic dialect. Although Smyrna and Chios early began competing for the honor (the poet Pindar, early in the 5th century BCE, associated Homer with both), and others joined in, no authenticated local memory survived anywhere of someone who, oral poet or not, must have been remarkable in his time.

Modern Inferences

Modern scholars agree with the ancient sources only about Homer's general place of activity. The most concrete piece of ancient evidence is that his descendants, the Homeridae, lived on the Ionic island of Chios.

Admittedly, there is some doubt over whether the *Iliad* and the *Odyssey* were even composed by the same main author. Such doubts began in antiquity itself and depended mainly on the difference of genre (the *Iliad* being martial and heroic, the *Odyssey* picaresque and often fantastic), but they may be reinforced by subtle differences of vocabulary even apart from those imposed by different subjects. The similarities of the two poems are partly due to the coherence of the heroic poetical tradition that lay behind both.

Partly on the basis of the internal evidence of the poems, which is of some use in determining when Homer lived, it seems plausible to conclude that the period of composition of the large-scale epics (as distinct from their much shorter predecessors) was the 9th or 8th century, with several features pointing more clearly to the 8th. The *Odyssey* may belong near the end of this century, the *Iliad* closer to its middle. It may be no coincidence that cults of Homeric heroes tended to spring up toward the end of the 8th century, and that scenes from the epic begin to appear on pots at just about the same time.

Homer as an Oral Poet

But even if his name is known and his date and region can be inferred, Homer remains primarily a projection of the great poems themselves. Their qualities are significant of his taste and his view of the world, but they also reveal something more specific about his technique and the kind of poet he was. Homeric tradition was an oral one: this was a kind of poetry made and passed down by word of mouth and without the intervention of writing. Indeed Homer's own term for a poet is *aoidos*, "singer." Ordinary *aoidoi*, whether resident at a royal court or performing at the invitation of a town's aristocracy, worked with relatively short poems that could be given completely on a single occasion. These poems must have provided the backbone of the tradition inherited by Homer. What Homer himself seems to have done is to introduce the concept of a quite different style of poetry, in the shape of a monumental poem that required more than a single hour or evening to sing and could achieve new and far more complex effects, in literary and psychological terms, than those attainable in the more anecdotal and episodic songs of his predecessors.

The Poems

Even apart from the possibilities of medium-scale elaboration, the *Iliad* and the *Odyssey* exemplify certain of the minor inconsistencies of all oral poetry, and occasionally the composer's amalgamation of traditional material into a large-scale structure shows through. Yet the overriding impression is one of powerful unity.

The *Iliad*—consisting of more than 16,000 verses, which would have taken four or five long evenings, and perhaps more, to perform—is not merely a distillation of the whole protracted war against Troy. It is simultaneously an exploration of the heroic ideal in all its self-contradictoriness—its insane and grasping pride, its magnificent but animal strength, its ultimate if obtuse humanity. The poem is, in truth, the story of the wrath of

Achilles, the greatest warrior on the Greek side, that is announced in its very first words. Yet for thousands of verses on end Achilles is an unseen presence. Much of the poetry between the first book, in which the quarrel flares up, and the 16th, in which Achilles makes the crucial concession of allowing his friend Patroclus to fight on his behalf, consists of long scenes of battle, in which individual encounters alternate with mass movements of the opposing armies. The battle poetry is based on typical and frequently recurring elements and motifs, but it is also subtly varied by highly individualized episodes and set pieces: the catalog of troop contingents, the formal duels between Paris and Menelaus and Ajax and Hector, Helen's identifying of the Achaean princes, and so on. Patroclus's death two-thirds of the way through the poem brings Achilles back into the fight. In book 22 he kills the deluded Hector. Next he restores his heroic status by means of the funeral games for Patroclus, and in the concluding book, Achilles is compelled by the gods to restore civilized values and his own magnanimity by surrendering Hector's body to King Priam.

The *Odyssey* tends to be blander in expression and sometimes more diffuse in the progress of its action, but it presents an even more complex and harmonious structure than the *Iliad*. The main elements include the situation in Ithaca, where Penelope, Odysseus's wife, and their young son, Telemachus, are powerless before her arrogant suitors as they despair of Odysseus's return from the siege of Troy, as well as Telemachus's secret journey to the Peloponnese for news of his father, and his encounters there with Nestor, Menelaus, and Helen. Odysseus's dangerous passage, opposed by the sea-god Poseidon himself, from Calypso's island to that of the Phaeacians, and his narrative of his fantastic adventures after leaving Troy, including his escape from the cave of the Cyclops, Polyphemus,

Although he is credited with writing two of the most famous poems, Homer is still a mysterious figure.

follows. His arrival back in Ithaca, solitary and by night, at the poem's halfway point, is followed by his meeting with his protector-goddess Athena, his elaborate disguises, his self-revelation to the faithful swineherd Eumaeus and then to Telemachus, their complicated plan for disposing of the suitors, and its gory fulfillment. Finally comes the recognition by his faithful Penelope, his recounting to her of his adventures, his meeting with his aged father, Laertes, and the restitution, with Athena's help, of stability in his island kingdom of Ithaca.

Homer's influence seems to have been strongest in some of the most conspicuous formal components of the poems. The participation of the gods can both dignify human events and make them seem trivial—or tragic. It must for long have been part of the heroic tradition, but the frequency and the richness of the divine assemblies in the *Iliad*, or the peculiarly personal and ambivalent relationship between Odysseus and Athena in the *Odyssey*, probably reflect the taste and capacity of the main composer. The *Iliad* and the *Odyssey* owe their unique status to the creative confluence of tradition and design, the crystalline fixity of a formulaic style, and the mobile spontaneity of a brilliant personal vision. The result is an impressive amalgam of literary power and refinement. The *Iliad* and the *Odyssey*, however, owe their preeminence not so much to their antiquity and to their place in Greek culture as a whole but to their timeless success in expressing, on a massive scale, so much of the triumph and the frustration of human life.

AESCHYLUS

(b. 525/524 BCE—d. 456/455 BCE, Gela, Sicily)

Aeschylus, the first of classical Athens's great dramatists, raised the emerging art of tragedy to great heights of poetry and theatrical power. He grew up in the turbulent period when the Athenian democracy, having thrown off its tyranny (the absolute rule of one man), had to prove itself against both self-seeking politicians at home and invaders from abroad. Aeschylus himself took part in his city's first struggles against the invading Persians. Later Greek chroniclers believed that Aeschylus was 35 years old in 490 BCE when he participated in the Battle of Marathon, in which the Athenians first repelled the Persians. If this is true, it would place his birth in 525 BCE. Aeschylus's father's name was Euphorion, and the family probably lived at Eleusis (west of Athens).

Aeschylus was a notable participant in Athens's major dramatic competition, the Great Dionysia, which was a part of the festival of Dionysus. He is recorded as having participated in this competition, probably for the first time, in 499 BCE. He won his first victory in the theater in the spring of 484 BCE. In the meantime, he had fought and possibly been wounded at Marathon, and Aeschylus singled out his participation in this battle years later for mention on the verse epitaph he wrote for himself. His brother was killed in this battle. In 480 BCE the Persians again invaded Greece, and once again Aeschylus saw service, fighting at the battles of Artemisium and Salamis. His responses to the Persian invasion found expression in his play *Persians*, the earliest of his works to survive. This play was produced in the competition of the spring of 472 BCE and won first prize.

Around this time Aeschylus is said to have visited Sicily to present *Persians* again at the tyrant Hieron I's court in Syracuse. Aeschylus's later career is a record of sustained dramatic success, though he is said to have suffered one memorable defeat, at the hands of the novice Sophocles, whose entry at the Dionysian festival of 468 BCE was victorious over the older poet's entry. Aeschylus recouped the loss with victory in the next year, 467, with his Oedipus trilogy (of which the third play, *Seven Against Thebes*, survives). After producing the masterpiece among his extant works, the *Oresteia* trilogy, in 458, Aeschylus went to Sicily again.

Aeschylus wrote approximately 90 plays, including satyr plays as well as tragedies; of these, about 80 titles are known. Only seven tragedies have survived entire. One account, perhaps based on the official lists, assigns Aeschylus 13 first prizes, or victories. This would mean that well over half of his plays won, since sets of four plays rather than separate ones were judged. According to the philosopher Flavius Philostratus, Aeschylus was known as the "Father of Tragedy."

Aeschylus's influence on the development of tragedy was fundamental. Previous to him, Greek drama was limited to one actor and a chorus engaged in a largely static recitation. (The chorus was a group of actors who responded to and commented on the main action of a play with song, dance, and recitation.) The actor could assume different roles by changing masks and costumes, but he was limited to engaging in dialogue only with the chorus. By adding a second actor with whom the first could converse, Aeschylus vastly increased the drama's possibilities for dialogue and dramatic tension and allowed more variety and freedom in plot construction. Although the dominance of the chorus in early tragedy is ultimately only hypothesis, it is probably true that, as Aristotle says in his *Poetics*, Aeschylus "reduced the chorus' role and made the plot the leading actor."

Aeschylus was an innovator in other ways as well. He made good use of stage settings and stage machinery, and some of his works were noted for their spectacular scenic effects. He also designed costumes, trained his choruses in their songs and dances, and probably acted in most of his own plays, this being the usual practice among Greek dramatists. But his formal innovations account for only part of his achievement. His plays are of lasting literary value in their majestic and compelling lyrical language, in the intricate architecture of their plots, and in the universal themes which they explore so honestly. Aeschylus's language in both dialogue and choral lyric is marked by force, majesty, and emotional intensity. He makes bold use of compound epithets, metaphors, and figurative turns of speech, but this rich language is firmly harnessed to the dramatic action rather than used as mere decoration.

Aeschylus is almost unequaled in writing tragedy that, for all its power of depicting evil and the fear and consequences of evil, ends, as in the *Oresteia*, in joy and reconciliation. Living at a time when the Greek people still truly felt themselves surrounded by the gods, Aeschylus nevertheless had a capacity for detached and general thought, which enabled him to treat the fundamental problem of evil with singular honesty and success.

The chronographers recorded Aeschylus's death at Gela (on Sicily's south coast) in 456/455, at age 69. A ludicrous story that he was killed when an eagle dropped a tortoise on his bald pate was presumably fabricated by a later comic writer. At Gela he was accorded a public funeral, with sacrifices and dramatic performances held at his grave, which subsequently became a place of pilgrimage for writers.

SOPHOCLES

(b. *c.* 496 BCE, Colonus, near Athens [Greece]—d. 406 BCE, Athens)

Sophocles, one of classical Athens's great tragic playwrights, was born in a village outside the walls of Athens, where his father, Sophillus, was a wealthy manufacturer of armor. Sophocles was wealthy from birth, highly educated, noted for his grace and charm, on easy terms with the leading families, and a personal friend of prominent statesmen. Because of his beauty of physique, his athletic prowess, and his skill in music, he was chosen in 480, when he was 16, to lead the paean (choral chant to a god) celebrating the decisive Greek sea victory over the Persians at the Battle of Salamis.

The relatively meager information about Sophocles' civic life suggests that he was a popular favorite who participated actively in his community and exercised outstanding artistic talents. In 442 he served as one of the treasurers responsible for receiving and managing tribute money from Athens's subject-allies in the Delian League. In 440 he was elected one of the 10 *stratēgoi* (high executive officials who commanded the armed forces) as a junior colleague of Pericles. Sophocles later served as *stratēgos* perhaps twice again. In 413, then aged about 83, Sophocles was a *proboulos*, one of 10 advisory commissioners who were granted special powers and were entrusted with organizing Athens's financial and domestic recovery after its terrible defeat at Syracuse in Sicily. These few facts, which are about all that is known of Sophocles' life, imply steady and distinguished attachment to Athens, its government, religion, and social forms.

Sophocles won his first victory at the Dionysian dramatic festival in 468, however, defeating the great Aeschylus in the process. This began a career of unparalleled success and longevity. In total, Sophocles wrote 123 dramas for the festivals. Since each author who was chosen to enter the competition usually presented four plays, this means he must have competed about 30 times. Sophocles won perhaps as many as 24 victories, compared to 13 for Aeschylus, and indeed he may have never received lower than second place in the competitions he entered.

Ancient authorities credit Sophocles with several major and minor dramatic innovations. Among the latter is his invention of some type of "scene paintings" or other pictorial prop to establish locale or atmosphere. He also may have increased the size of the chorus from 12 to 15 members. Sophocles' major innovation was his introduction of a third actor into the dramatic performance. It had previously been permissible for two actors to "double" (i.e., assume other roles during a play), but the addition of a third actor onstage enabled the dramatist both to increase the number of his characters and widen the variety of their interactions. The scope of the dramatic conflict was thereby extended, plots could be more fluid, and situations could be more complex.

The typical Sophoclean drama presents a few characters, impressive in their determination and power, and possessing a few strongly drawn qualities or faults that combine with a particular set of circumstances to lead them inevitably to a tragic fate. Sophocles develops his characters' rush to tragedy with great economy, concentration, and dramatic effectiveness, creating a coherent, suspenseful situation whose sustained and inexorable onrush came to epitomize the tragic form to the classical world. Sophocles emphasizes that most people lack wisdom, and he presents truth in collision with ignorance, delusion, and folly. Many scenes dramatize flaws or failure in thinking (deceptive reports and rumors, false optimism, hasty judgment, madness). The chief character does something involving grave error; this affects others, each of whom reacts in his own way, thereby causing the chief agent to take another step toward ruin—his own and that of others as well. Equally important, those who are to suffer from the tragic error usually are present at the time or belong to the same generation. It was this more complex type of tragedy that demanded a third actor. Sophocles thus abandoned the spacious Aeschylean framework of the connected trilogy and instead comprised the entire action in a single play.

Sophocles' language responds flexibly to the dramatic needs of the moment. It can be ponderously weighty or swift-moving, emotionally intense or easygoing, highly decorative or perfectly plain and simple. His mastery of form and diction was highly respected by his contemporaries. Sophocles has also been admired for the sympathy and vividness with which he delineates his characters; especially notable are his tragic women, such as Electra and Antigone. Few dramatists have been able to handle situation and plot with more power and certainty; the frequent references in the *Poetics* to Sophocles' *Oedipus the King* show that Aristotle regarded this play as a masterpiece of construction, and few later critics have dissented. Sophocles is also unsurpassed in his moments of high dramatic tension and in his revealing use of tragic irony.

In one of his last plays, *Oedipus at Colonus*, he still affectionately praises both his own birthplace and the great city itself. Sophocles' last recorded act was to lead a chorus in public mourning for his deceased rival, Euripides, before the festival of 406. He died that same year.

ARISTOPHANES

(b. *c.* 450 BCE—d. *c.* 388 BCE)

Aristophanes is the greatest representative of ancient Greek comedy, and the one whose works have been preserved in greatest quantity. He is the only extant representative of the Old Comedy, that is, of the phase of comic dramaturgy in which chorus, mime, and burlesque still played a considerable part and which was characterized by bold fantasy, merciless invective and outrageous satire, unabashedly licentious humor, and a marked freedom of political criticism. But Aristophanes belongs to the end of this phase, and, indeed, his last extant play, which has no choric element at all, may well be regarded as the only extant specimen of the short-lived Middle Comedy, which, before the end of the 4th century BCE, was to be superseded in turn by the milder and more realistic social satire of the New Comedy.

Little is known about the life of Aristophanes, and most of the known facts are derived from references in his own plays. He was an Athenian citizen belonging to the *deme*, or clan, named Pandionis, but his actual birthplace is uncertain. (The fact that he or his father, Philippus, owned property on the island of Aegina may have been the cause of an accusation by his fellow citizens that he was not of Athenian birth.) He began his dramatic career in 427 BCE with a play, the *Daitaleis* (*The Banqueters*), which appears, from surviving fragments, to have been a satire on his contemporaries' educational and moral theories. He is thought to have written about 40 plays in all.

A large part of his work is concerned with the social, literary, and philosophical life of Athens itself and with themes provoked by the great Peloponnesian War (431–404 BCE). This war was essentially a conflict between imperialist Athens and conservative Sparta, and so was long the dominant issue in Athenian politics. Aristophanes was naturally an opponent of the more or less bellicose statesmen who controlled the government of Athens throughout the better part of his maturity. Aristophanes lived to see the revival of Athens after its defeat by Sparta.

Aristophanes' reputation has stood the test of time. His plays have been frequently produced on the 20th- and 21st-century stage in numerous translations, which manage with varying degrees of success to convey the flavor of Aristophanes' puns, witticisms, and topical allusions. But it is not easy to say why his comedies still appeal to an audience more than two millennia after they were written. In the matter of plot construction, Aristophanes' comedies are often loosely put together, are full of inconsequential episodes, and often degenerate at their end into a series of disconnected and boisterous episodes. Aristophanes' greatness lies in the wittiness of his dialogue; his generally good-humored though occasionally malevolent satire; the brilliance of his parody, especially when he mocks the controversial tragedian Euripides; the ingenuity and inventiveness, not to say the laughable absurdity, of his comic scenes born of imaginative fantasy; the peculiar charm of his choric songs, whose freshness can still be conveyed in languages other than Greek; and, at least for audiences of a permissive age, the licentious frankness of many scenes and allusions in his comedies. Among his plays are *Wasps* (422 BCE), which satirized the litigiousness of the Athenians in the person of a mean and waspish old man who has a passion for serving on juries, and *Lysistrata* (411 BCE), in which the women of Athens seize the Acropolis and the city's treasury and declare a sex strike until such time as the men will make peace. *Lysistrata* achieves a mixture of humor, indecency, gravity, and farce that marks many of Aristophanes' plays.

GAIUS VALERIUS CATULLUS

(b. *c.* 84 BCE, Verona, Cisalpine Gaul—d. *c.* 54 BCE, Rome)

Gaius Valerius Catullus was a Roman poet whose expressions of love and hatred are generally considered the finest lyric poetry of ancient Rome.

No ancient biography of Catullus survives. A few facts can be pieced together from external sources and in the works of his contemporaries or of later writers, supplemented by inferences drawn from his poems, some of which are certain, some only possible. Catullus was alive

55–54 BCE on the evidence of four of his poems, and died young, according to the poet Ovid—at the age of 30 as stated by St. Jerome (writing about the end of the 4th century), who nevertheless dated his life erroneously 87–57 BCE. Catullus was thus a contemporary of the statesmen Cicero, Pompey, and Julius Caesar, who are variously addressed by him in his poems. He preceded the poets of the immediately succeeding age of the emperor Augustus, among whom Horace, Sextus Propertius, Tibullus, and Ovid name him as a poet whose work is familiar to them. Catullus owned property at Sirmio, the modern Sirmione, on Lake Garda, though he preferred to live in Rome and owned a villa near the Roman suburb of Tibur, in an unfashionable neighborhood.

In a poem externally datable to *c.* 57–56 BCE, Catullus reports one event, a journey to Bithynia in Asia Minor in the retinue of Gaius Memmius, the Roman governor of the province, from which he returned to Sirmio. His poetry also records two emotional crises, the death of a brother whose grave he visited in the Troad, also in Asia Minor, and an intense and unhappy love affair, portrayed variously in 25 poems, with a woman who was married and whom he names Lesbia, a pseudonym (Ovid states) for Clodia, according to the 2nd-century writer Apuleius. (She may have been a patrician, one of the three Clodia sisters of Cicero's foe Publius Clodius Pulcher. All three were the subject of scandalous rumor, according to Plutarch.) His poems also record, directly or indirectly, a homosexual affair with a youth named Juventius.

Among his longer poems are two marriage hymns; one romantic narrative in hexameters (lines of six feet) on the marriage of Peleus with the sea goddess Thetis; and four elegiac pieces, consisting of an epistle introducing a translation of an elegant conceit by the Alexandrian poet Callimachus, followed by a pasquinade, or scurrilous conversation, between the poet and a door, and lastly a soliloquy addressed to a friend and cast in the form of an encomium, or poem of praise.

In his lifetime, Catullus was a poet's poet, addressing himself to fellow craftsmen (*docti*, or scholarly poets), especially to his friend Licinius Calvus, who is often posthumously commemorated along with him. The conversational rhythms of his poetry, as he managed them for lyric purposes, achieved an immediacy that no other classic poet can rival. For the general reader, the 25 Lesbia poems are likely to remain the most memorable, recording as they do a love that could register ecstasy and despair and all the divided emotions that intervene. Two of them with unusual meter recall Sappho, the poet of the Aegean island of Lesbos, as also does his use of the pseudonym Lesbia. The quality of his poems of invective, which spare neither Caesar nor otherwise unknown personalities, is uneven, ranging from the high-spirited to the tedious, from the lapidary to the labored. But their satiric humor is often effective, and their obscenity reflects a serious literary convention that the poet himself defends.

VIRGIL

(b. Oct. 15, 70 BCE, Andes, near Mantua [Italy]—d. Sept. 21, 19 BCE, Brundisium)

The Roman poet Virgil, best known for his national epic, the *Aeneid* (from *c.* 30 BCE), was regarded by the Romans as their greatest poet, an estimation that subsequent generations have upheld. His fame rests chiefly upon the *Aeneid*, which tells the story of Rome's legendary founder and proclaims the Roman mission to civilize the world under divine guidance.

Early Life

Virgil, whose Latin name was Publius Vergilius Maro, was born of peasant stock. He was educated at Cremona, at Milan, and finally at Rome, acquiring a thorough knowledge of Greek and Roman authors, especially of the poets, and receiving a detailed training in rhetoric and philosophy.

During Virgil's youth, as the Roman Republic neared its end, the political and military situation in Italy was confused and often calamitous. The civil war between Marius and Sulla had been succeeded by conflict between Pompey and Julius Caesar for supreme power. When Virgil was 20, Caesar with his armies swooped south from Gaul, crossed the Rubicon, and began the series of civil wars that were not to end until Augustus's victory at Actium in 31 BCE. Hatred and fear of civil war is powerfully expressed by both Virgil and his contemporary Horace.

Virgil's life was devoted entirely to his poetry and studies connected with it. His health was never robust, and he played no part in military or political life. It is said that he spoke once in the law courts without distinction and that his shy and retiring nature caused him to give up any ideas he might have had of taking part in the world of affairs. He never married, and the first half of his life was that of a scholar and near recluse. But, as his poetry won him fame, he gradually won the friendship of many important men in the Roman world.

Literary Career

Virgil's earliest certain work is the *Eclogues*, a collection of 10 pastoral poems composed between 42 and 37 BCE. Some of them are escapist, literary excursions to the idyllic pastoral world of Arcadia based on the Greek poet

Theocritus (fl. *c.* 280 BCE) but more unreal and stylized. One eclogue in particular stands out as having relevance to the contemporary situation, and this is the fourth (sometimes called the Messianic, because it was later regarded as prophetic of Christianity). It is an elevated poem, prophesying in sonorous and mystic terms the birth of a child who will bring back the Golden Age, banish sin, and restore peace. It was clearly written at a time when the clouds of civil war seemed to be lifting; it can be dated firmly to 41–40 BCE. It seems most likely that Virgil refers to an expected child of the triumvir Antony and his wife Octavia, sister of Octavian. But, though a specific occasion may be allocated to the poem, it goes beyond the particular and, in symbolic terms, presents a vision of world harmony, which was, to some extent, destined to be realized under Augustus.

One of the most disastrous effects of the civil wars—and one of which Virgil, as a countryman, would be most intensely aware—was the depopulation of rural Italy. The farmers had been obliged to go to war, and their farms fell into neglect and ruin as a result. The *Georgics*, composed between 37 and 30 BCE (the final period of the civil wars), is a plea for the restoration of the traditional agricultural life of Italy. It is dedicated to Maecenas, one of the chief of Augustus's ministers, who was also the leading patron of the arts. By this time Virgil was a member of what might be called the court circle, and his desire to see his beloved Italy restored to its former glories coincided with the national requirement of resettling the land and diminishing the pressure on the cities. It would be wrong to think of Virgil as writing political propaganda; but equally it would be wrong to regard his poetry as unconnected with the major currents of political and social needs of the time. Virgil was personally committed to the same ideals.

Virgil is considered to be one of the greatest poets of ancient Rome.

In the year 31 BCE, when Virgil was 38, Augustus (still known as Octavian) won the final battle of the civil wars at Actium against the forces of Antony and Cleopatra. Virgil, like many of his contemporaries, felt a great sense of relief that the civil strife was at last over and was deeply grateful to the man who had made it possible. Augustus was anxious to preserve the traditions of the republic and its constitutional forms, but he was in fact sole ruler of the Roman world. He used his power to establish a period of peace and stability and endeavored to reawaken in the Romans a sense of national pride and a new enthusiasm for their ancestral religion and their traditional moral values (bravery, parsimony, duty, responsibility, and family devotion). Virgil, too, felt a deep attachment to the simple virtues and religious traditions of the Italian people. All his life he had been preparing himself to write an epic poem (regarded then as the highest form of poetic achievement), and he now set out to embody his ideal Rome in the *Aeneid*, the story of the foundation of the first settlement in Italy, from which Rome was to spring, by an exiled Trojan prince after the destruction of Troy by the Greeks in the 12th century BCE.

The theme he chose gave him two great advantages. One was that its date and subject were very close to those of Homer's *Iliad* and *Odyssey*, so that Virgil could remodel episodes and characters from his great Greek predecessor. The other was that it could be brought into relationship with his contemporary Augustan world by presenting Aeneas as the prototype of the Roman way of life (the last of the Trojans and the first of the Romans). Moreover, by the use of prophecies and visions and devices such as the description of the pictures on Aeneas's shield or of the origins of contemporary customs and institutions, it could foreshadow the real events of Roman history.

The real greatness of the *Aeneid* is due to Virgil's awareness of the private, as well as the public, aspects of human life. The *Aeneid* is no panegyric; it sets the achievements and aspirations of the giant organization of Roman governmental rule in tension with the frustrated hopes and sufferings of individuals. The most memorable figure in the poem—and, it has been said, the only character to be created by a Roman poet that has passed into world literature—is Dido, Queen of Carthage, opponent of the Roman way of life. In a mere panegyric of Rome, she could have been presented in such a way that Aeneas's rejection of her would have been a victory to applaud. In fact, in the fourth book she wins so much sympathy that the reader wonders whether Rome should be bought at this price.

The *Aeneid* occupied Virgil for 11 years and, at his death, had not yet received its final revision. In 19 BCE, planning to spend a further three years on his poem, he set out for Greece—doubtless to obtain local color for the revision of those parts of the *Aeneid* set in Greek waters. On the voyage he caught a fever and returned to Italy but died soon after arrival at Brundisium. Whether the *Aeneid* would have undergone major changes cannot be guessed. The story goes that Virgil's dying wish was for his poem to be burned, but that this request was countermanded by the order of Augustus.

IMRU' AL-QAYS

(d. *c.* 500 CE)

The Arab poet Imru' al-Qays was acknowledged as the most distinguished poet of pre-Islamic times by the Prophet Muhammad, by ʿAlī, the fourth caliph, and by Arab critics of the ancient Basra school. He is the author of one of the seven odes in the famed collection of pre-

Islamic poetry *Al-Muʿallaqāt*.

There is no agreement as to his genealogy, but the predominant legend cites Imruʾ al-Qays as the youngest son of Ḥujr, the last king of Kindah. He was twice expelled from his father's court for the erotic poetry he was fond of writing, and he assumed the life of a vagabond. After his father was murdered by a rebel Bedouin tribe, the Banū Asad, Imruʾ al-Qays was single-minded in his pursuit of revenge. He successfully attacked and routed the Banū Asad, but, unsatisfied, he went from tribe to tribe fruitlessly seeking further help. Through King al-Ḥārith of Ghassān (northern Arabia), Imruʾ al-Qays was introduced to the Byzantine emperor Justinian I, who agreed to supply him with the troops that he needed to regain his kingdom. Legend has it that on his return to Arabia the emperor sent him a poisoned cloak, which caused his death at Ancyra (modern Ankara).

The philologists of the Basra school regarded Imruʾ al-Qays not only as the greatest of the poets of the *Muʿallaqāt* but also as the inventor of the form of the classical ode, or *qaṣīdah*, and of many of its conventions, such as the poet's weeping over the traces of deserted campsites. The opening of the long *qaṣīdah* by Imruʾ al-Qays that appears in the *Muʿallaqāt* is perhaps the best-known line of poetry in Arabic: "Halt, you two companions, and let us weep for the memory of a beloved and an abode mid the sand-dunes between Al-Dakhūl and Ḥawmal."

The hunting scenes and bluntly erotic narratives by Imruʾ al-Qays in the *Muʿallaqāt* represent important early precedents of the genres of hunt poetry and love poetry in Arabic literature. There were at least three collections (divans) of his poetry made by medieval Arab scholars, numbering as many as 68 poems. The authenticity of the greater part of them, however, is doubtful.

DU FU

(b. 712, Gongxian, Henan province, China—d. 770, on a riverboat between Danzhou [now Changsha] and Yueyang, Hunan province)

Du Fu is considered by many literary critics to be the greatest Chinese poet of all time, rivaled in that designation only by his contemporary Li Bai.

Born into a scholarly family, Du Fu received a traditional Confucian education but failed in the imperial examinations of 735. As a result, he spent much of his youth traveling. During his travels he won renown as a poet and met other poets of the period, including the great Li Bai, the unofficial poet laureate to the military expedition of Prince Lin, who was arrested when the prince was accused of intending to establish an independent kingdom and was executed. After a brief flirtation with Daoism while traveling with Li Bai, Du Fu returned to the capital and to the conventional Confucianism of his youth. He never again met Li Bai, despite his strong admiration for his freewheeling contemporary.

During the 740s Du Fu was a well-regarded member of a group of high officials, even though he was without money and official position himself and failed a second time in an imperial examination. He married, probably in 741. Between 751 and 755 he tried to attract imperial attention by submitting a succession of literary products that were couched in a language of ornamental flattery, a device that eventually resulted in a nominal position at court.

In 755, during An Lushan's rebellion, Du Fu experienced extreme personal hardships. He escaped them, however, and in 757 joined the exiled court, being given the position of censor. His memoranda to the emperor do not appear to have been particularly welcome; he was eventually relieved of his post and endured another period of poverty and hunger. Wandering about until the mid-760s, he briefly served a local warlord, a position that enabled him to acquire some land and to become a gentleman farmer, but in 768 he again started traveling aimlessly toward the south. Popular legend attributes his death (on a riverboat on the Xiang River) to overindulgence in food and wine after a 10-day fast.

Du Fu's early poetry celebrated the beauty of the natural world and bemoaned the passage of time. He soon began to write bitingly of war—seen in *Bingqu xing* (*The Ballad of the Army Carts*), a poem about conscription—and with hidden satire, as in *Liren xing* (*The Beautiful Woman*), which speaks of the conspicuous luxury of the court. As he matured, and especially during the tumultuous period of 755 to 759, his verse began to sound a note of profound compassion for humanity caught in the grip of senseless war.

Du Fu's paramount position in the history of Chinese literature rests on his superb classicism. He was highly erudite, and his intimate acquaintance with the literary tradition of the past was equaled only by his complete ease in handling the rules of prosody. His dense, compressed language makes use of all the connotative overtones of a phrase and of all the intonational potentials of the individual word, qualities that no translation can ever reveal. He was an expert in all poetic genres current in his day, but his mastery was at its height in the *lüshi*, or "regulated verse," which he refined to a point of glowing intensity.

AL-MUTANABBI

(b. 915, Kūfah, Iraq—d. Sept. 23, 965, near Dayr al- ʿĀqūl)

Al-Mutanabbī, regarded by many as the greatest poet of the Arabic language, primarily wrote panegyrics in a flowery, bombastic, and highly influential style marked by improbable metaphors.

Al-Mutanabbī was the son of a water carrier who claimed noble and ancient southern Arabian descent. Because of his poetic talent, al-Mutanabbī received an education. When Shī'ite Qarmatians sacked Kūfah in 924, he joined them and lived among the Bedouin, learning their doctrines and Arabic. Claiming to be a prophet—hence the name al-Mutanabbī ("The Would-Be Prophet")—he led a Qarmatian revolt in Syria in 932. After its suppression and two years' imprisonment, he recanted in 935 and became a wandering poet.

He began to write panegyrics in the tradition established by the poets Abū Tammām and al-Buḥturī. A panegyric on the military victories of Sayf al-Dawlah, the Ḥamdānid poet-prince of northern Syria, resulted in al-Mutanabbī's attaching himself to the ruler's court in 948. During his time there, al-Mutanabbī lauded his patron in panegyrics that rank as masterpieces of Arabic poetry. Among his lines of praise for Sayf al-Dawlah are ones written after the prince's recovery from illness: "Light is now returned to the sun; previously it was extinguished / As though the lack of it in a body were a kind of disease."

The latter part of this period was clouded with intrigues and jealousies that culminated in al-Mutanabbī's leaving Syria in 957 for Egypt, then ruled in name by the Ikhshīdids. Al-Mutanabbī attached himself to the regent, the Ethiopian eunuch Abū al-Misk Kāfūr, who had been born a slave. But he offended Kāfūr by lampooning him in scurrilous satirical poems and fled Egypt about 960. After further travels—including to Baghdad, where he was unable to secure patronage, and to Kūfah, where he again defended the city from attack by the Qarmatians—al-Mutanabbī lived in Shīrāz, Iran, under the protection of the emir 'Aḍūd al-Dawlah of the Būyid dynasty until

965, when he returned to Iraq and was killed by bandits near Baghdad.

Al-Mutanabbī's pride and arrogance set the tone for much of his verse, which is ornately rhetorical yet crafted with consummate skill and artistry. He gave to the traditional *qaṣīdah*, or ode, a freer and more personal development, writing in what can be called a neoclassical style that combined some elements of Iraqi and Syrian stylistics with classical features.

FERDOWSI

(b. *c.* 935, near Ṭūs, Iran—d. *c.* 1020–26, Ṭūs)

Ferdowsī was a Persian poet who gave to the *Shāh-nāmeh* ("Book of Kings"), the Persian national epic, its final and enduring form.

He was born in a village on the outskirts of the ancient city of Ṭūs. In the course of the centuries many legends have been woven around the poet's name—which is itself the pseudonym of Abū al-Qasem Manṣūr—but very little else, other than his birthplace, is known about the real facts of his life. The only reliable source is given by Neẓāmī-ye ʿArūẓī, a 12th-century poet who visited Ferdowsī's tomb in 1116 or 1117 and collected the traditions that were current in his birthplace less than a century after his death.

According to Neẓāmī, Ferdowsī was a *dehqān* ("landowner"), deriving a comfortable income from his estates. He had only one child, a daughter, and it was to provide her with a dowry that he set his hand to the task that was to occupy him for 35 years. The *Shāh-nāmeh* of Ferdowsī, a poem of nearly 60,000 couplets, is based mainly on a prose work of the same name compiled in the poet's early manhood in his native Ṭūs. This prose *Shāh-nāmeh* was in turn and for the most part the translation of a Pahlavi (Middle Persian) work, the *Khvatāy-nāmak*, a history of the kings of Persia from mythical times down to the reign of Khosrow II (590–628). It also contained additional material continuing the story to the overthrow of the Sāsānians by the Arabs in the middle of the 7th century. The first to undertake the versification of this chronicle of pre-Islāmic and legendary Persia was Daqīqī, a poet at the court of the Sāmānids, who came to a violent end after completing only 1,000 verses. These verses, which deal with the rise of the prophet Zoroaster, were afterward incorporated by Ferdowsī, with due acknowledgements, in his own poem.

The *Shāh-nāmeh*, finally completed in 1010, was presented to the celebrated sultan Maḥmūd of Ghazna, who by that time had made himself master of Ferdowsī's homeland, Khūrāsān. Information on the relations between poet and patron is largely legendary. According to Neẓāmī-ye ʿArūẓī, Ferdowsī came to Ghazna in person and through the good offices of the minister Aḥmad ebn Ḥasan Meymandī was able to secure the Sultan's acceptance of the poem. Unfortunately, Maḥmūd then consulted certain enemies of the minister as to the poet's reward. They suggested that Ferdowsī should be given 50,000 dirhams, and even this, they said, was too much, in view of his heretical Shī'īte tenets. Maḥmūd, a bigoted Sunnite, was influenced by their words, and in the end Ferdowsī received only 20,000 dirhams. Bitterly disappointed, he went to the bath and, on coming out, bought a draft of *foqāʿ* (a kind of beer) and divided the whole of the money between the bath attendant and the seller of *foqāʿ*.

Fearing the Sultan's wrath, he fled first to Herāt, where he was in hiding for six months, and then, by way of his native Ṭūs, to Mazanderan, where he found refuge at the court of the Sepahbād Shahreyār, whose family claimed descent from the last of the Sāsānians. There Ferdowsī composed a satire of 100 verses on Sultan Maḥmūd that he inserted in the preface of the *Shāh-nāmeh* and read it to Shahreyār, at the same time offering to dedicate the poem to him, as a descendant of the ancient kings of Persia, instead of to Maḥmūd. Shahreyār, however, persuaded him to leave the dedication to Maḥmūd, bought the satire from him for 1,000 dirhams a verse, and had it expunged from the poem. The whole text of this satire, bearing every mark of authenticity, has survived to the present.

It was long supposed that in his old age the poet had spent some time in western Persia or even in Baghdad under the protection of the Būyids, but this assumption was based upon his presumed authorship of *Yūsof o-Zalīkhā*, an epic poem on the subject of Joseph and Potiphar's wife, which, it later became known, was composed more than 100 years after Ferdowsī's death. According to the narrative of Neẓāmī-ye ʿArūẓī, Ferdowsī died inopportunely just as Sultan Maḥmūd had determined to make amends for his shabby treatment of the poet by sending him 60,000 dinars' worth of indigo. Neẓāmī does not mention the date of Ferdowsī's death. The earliest date given by later authorities is 1020 and the latest 1026; it is certain that he lived to be more than 80.

The Persians regard Ferdowsī as the greatest of their poets. For nearly a thousand years they have continued to read and to listen to recitations from his masterwork, the *Shāh-nāmeh*, in which the Persian national epic found its final and enduring form. Though written about 1,000 years ago, this work is as intelligible to the average, modern Iranian as the King James version of the Bible is to a modern English-speaker. The language, based as the poem is on a Pahlavi original, is pure Persian with only the slightest admixture of Arabic. European scholars have criticized this enormous poem for what they have regarded as its monotonous meter, its constant repetitions, and its stereotyped similes; but to the Iranian it is the history of his country's glorious past, preserved for all time in sonorous and majestic verse.

MURASAKI SHIKIBU

(b. *c.* 978, Kyōto, Japan—d. *c.* 1014, Kyōto)

Murasaki Shikibu is the name that has been given to the court lady who was the author of the *Genji monogatari* (*The Tale of Genji*), generally considered the greatest work of Japanese literature and thought to be the world's oldest full novel. Her real name, however, is unknown; it is conjectured that she acquired the sobriquet of Murasaki from the name of the heroine of her novel. The main source of knowledge about her life is the diary she kept between 1007 and 1010. This work possesses considerable interest for the delightful glimpses it affords of life at the court of the empress Jōtō mon'in, whom Murasaki Shikibu served.

Some critics believe that she wrote the entire *Tale of Genji* between 1001 (the year her husband, Fujiwara Nobutaka, died) and 1005, when she began serving at court. More probably, however, the composition of this extremely long and complex novel extended over a much greater period and was not finished until about 1010.

The Tale of Genji captures the image of a unique society of ultrarefined and elegant aristocrats, whose indispensable accomplishments were skill in poetry, music, calligraphy, and courtship. Much of it is concerned with the loves of Prince Genji and the different women in his life, all of whom are exquisitely delineated. Although the novel does not contain scenes of powerful action, it is permeated with a sensitivity to human emotions and to the beauties of nature hardly paralleled elsewhere. The tone of the novel darkens as it progresses, indicating perhaps a deepening of Murasaki Shikibu's Buddhist conviction of the vanity of the world. Some, however, believe that its last 14 chapters were written by another author. The translation (1935) of *The Tale of Genji* by Arthur Waley is a classic of English literature. Murasaki Shikibu's diary is included in *Diaries of Court Ladies of Old Japan* (1935), translated by Annie Shepley Ōmori and Kōchi Doi.

RUMI

(b. *c.* Sept. 30, 1207, Balkh [now in Afghanistan]—d. Dec. 17, 1273)

Jalāl al-Dīn Rūmī, the greatest Sufi mystic and poet in the Persian language, is famous for his lyrics and for his didactic epic *Mas̄navī-yi Maʿnavī* ("Spiritual Couplets"), which widely influenced mystical thought and literature throughout the Muslim world. After his death, his disciples were organized as the Mawlawīyah order.

Jalāl al-Dīn's father, Bahāʾ al-Dīn Walad, was a noted mystical theologian, author, and teacher. Because of either a dispute with the ruler or the threat of the approaching Mongols, Bahāʾ al-Dīn and his family left their native town in about 1218. According to legend, in Nīshāpūr, Iran, the family met Farīd al-Dīn ʿAṭṭār, a Persian mystical poet, who blessed young Jalāl al-Dīn. After a pilgrimage to Mecca and journeys through the Middle East, Bahāʾ al-Dīn and his family reached Anatolia (Rūm, hence the surname Rūmī), a region that enjoyed peace and prosperity under the rule of the Turkish Seljuq dynasty. After a short stay at Laranda (Karaman), where Jalāl al-Dīn's mother died and his first son was born, they were called to the capital, Konya, in 1228. Here, Bahāʾ al-Dīn Walad taught at one of the numerous madrasahs (religious schools); after his death in 1231 he was succeeded in this capacity by his son.

A year later, Burhān al-Dīn Muḥaqqiq, one of Bahā' al-Dīn's former disciples, arrived in Konya and acquainted Jalāl al-Dīn more deeply with some mystical theories that had developed in Iran. Burhān al-Dīn, who contributed considerably to Jalāl al-Dīn's spiritual formation, left Konya about 1240. Jalāl al-Dīn is said to have undertaken one or two journeys to Syria (unless his contacts with Syrian Sufi circles were already established before his family reached Anatolia); there he may have met Ibn al-'Arabī, the leading Islamic theosophist whose interpreter and stepson, Ṣadr al-Dīn al-Qunawī, was Jalāl al-Dīn's colleague and friend in Konya.

The decisive moment in Rūmī's life occurred on November 30, 1244, when in the streets of Konya he met the wandering dervish—holy man—Shams al-Dīn (Sun of Religion) of Tabrīz, whom he may have first encountered in Syria. Shams al-Dīn cannot be connected with any of the traditional mystical fraternities. His overwhelming personality, however, revealed to Jalāl al-Dīn the mysteries of divine majesty and beauty. For months the two mystics lived closely together, and Rūmī neglected his disciples and family so that his scandalized entourage forced Shams to leave the town in February 1246. Jalāl al-Dīn was heartbroken; his eldest son, Sulṭān Walad, eventually brought Shams back from Syria. The family, however, could not tolerate the close relation of Jalāl al-Dīn with his beloved, and one night in 1247 Shams disappeared forever. In the 20th century it was established that Shams was indeed murdered, not without the knowledge of Rūmī's sons, who hurriedly buried him close to a well that is still extant in Konya.

This experience of love, longing, and loss turned Rūmī into a poet. His poems—*ghazals* (about 30,000 verses) and a large number of *robāʿīyāt* ("quatrains")—reflect the different stages of his love, until, as his son writes, "he found Shams in himself, radiant like the moon." The complete identification of lover and beloved is expressed by his inserting the name of Shams instead of his own pen name at the end of most of his lyrical poems. The *Dīvān-e Shams* ("The Collected Poetry of Shams") is a true translation of his experiences into poetry; its language, however, never becomes lost in lofty spiritual heights or nebulous speculation. The fresh language, propelled by its strong rhythms, sometimes assumes forms close to popular verses. There would seem to be cause for the belief, expressed by chroniclers, that much of this poetry was composed in a state of ecstasy, induced by the music of the flute or the drum, the hammering of the goldsmiths, or the sound of the water mill in Meram, where Rūmī used to go with his disciples to enjoy nature. He found in nature the reflection of the radiant beauty of the Sun of Religion and felt flowers and birds partaking in his love. He often accompanied his verses by a whirling dance, and many of his poems were composed to be sung in Sufi musical gatherings.

A few years after Shams al-Dīn's death, Rūmī experienced a similar rapture in his acquaintance with an illiterate goldsmith, Ṣālāḥ al-Dīn Zarkūb. It is said that one day, hearing the sound of a hammer in front of Ṣalāḥ al-Dīn's shop in the bazaar of Konya, Rūmī began his dance. The shop owner had long been one of Rūmī's closest and most loyal disciples, and his daughter became the wife of Rūmī's eldest son. This love again inspired Rūmī to write poetry. After Ṣālāḥ al-Dīn's death, Ḥusām al-Dīn Chelebi became his spiritual love and deputy. Rūmī's main work, the *Maš̄navī-yi Maʿnavī*, was composed under his influence. Ḥusām al-Dīn had asked him to follow the model of the poets ʿAṭṭār and Sanā'i, who had laid down mystical teachings in long poems, interspersed with anecdotes, fables, stories, proverbs, and allegories. Their works were widely read by the mystics and by Rūmī's disciples. Rūmī followed Ḥusām al-Dīn's advice and composed nearly 26,000 couplets of the *Masnavī* during the following years. It is said that he would recite his verses even in the bath or on the roads, accompanied by Ḥusām al-Dīn, who wrote them down. The *Masnavī* shows all the different aspects of Sufism in the 13th century, and it reflects the experience of divine love; both Ṣalāḥ al-Dīn and Ḥusām al-Dīn were, for Rūmī, renewed manifestations of Shams al-Dīn, the all-embracing light.

Rūmī lived for a short while after completing the *Masnavī*. He always remained a respected member of Konya society, and his company was sought by the leading officials as well as by Christian monks. Ḥusām al-Dīn was his successor and was in turn succeeded by Sulṭān Walad, who organized the loose fraternity of Rūmī's disciples into the Mawlawīyah, known in the West as the Whirling Dervishes because of the mystical dance that constitutes their principal ritual. Sulṭān Walad's poetical accounts of his father's life are the most important source of knowledge of Rūmī's spiritual development. His mausoleum, the Green Dome, today a museum in Konya, is still a place of pilgrimage for thousands of all faiths from around the world.

DANTE

(b. *c.* May 21–June 20, 1265, Florence, Italy—d. Sept. 13/14, 1321, Ravenna)

Dante Alighieri was an Italian poet, prose writer, literary theorist, moral philosopher, and political thinker who is best known for the monumental epic poem *La commedia*, later named *La divina commedia* (*The Divine Comedy*).

Public Career and Exile

Dante was of noble ancestry, and his life was shaped by the conflict between the papal and imperial partisans called, respectively, Guelfs and Ghibellines. When an opposing political faction within the Guelfs (Dante's party) gained ascendancy in Florence, he was called in January 1302 to appear before the new government and, failing to do so, was condemned for crimes he had not committed. Again failing to appear some weeks later, Dante and others within his party were condemned to be burned to death. He soon after went into exile and never again returned to Florence.

His great friendship with the poet Guido Cavalcanti shaped Dante's later career. More important, however, was Beatrice, a figure in whom Dante created one of the most celebrated fictionalized women in all of literature. *La vita nuova* (*c.* 1293; *The New Life*) tells a simple story: Dante's first sight of Beatrice when both are nine years of age, her salutation when they are 18, Dante's expedients to conceal his love for her, the crisis experienced when Beatrice withholds her greeting, Dante's anguish that she is making light of him, his determination to rise above anguish and sing only of his lady's virtues, anticipations of her death, and finally the death of Beatrice, Dante's mourning, the temptation of the sympathetic *donna gentile* (a young woman who temporarily replaces Beatrice), Beatrice's final triumph and apotheosis, and, in the last chapter, Dante's determination to write at some later time about her "that which has never been written of any woman." Yet with all of this apparently autobiographical purpose, the *Vita nuova* is strangely impersonal. The circumstances it sets down are markedly devoid of any historical facts or descriptive detail (thus making it pointless to engage in too much debate as to the exact historical identity of Beatrice).

This 1465 painting by Domenico di Michelino memorializes the poet Dante.

Vita nuova is the first of two collections of verse that Dante made in his lifetime, the other being the *Il convivio* (*c.* 1304–07; *The Banquet*). Each is a *prosimetrum*, that is, a work composed of verse and prose. In each case the prose is a device for binding together poems composed over about a 10-year period. The *Vita nuova* brought together Dante's poetic efforts from before 1283 to roughly 1292–93; the *Convivio*, a bulkier and more ambitious work, contains Dante's most important poetic compositions from just prior to 1294 to the time of *The Divine Comedy*.

The *Convivio* was among the works he wrote during his difficult years of exile. In it Dante's mature political and philosophical system is nearly complete. He makes his first stirring defense of the imperial tradition and, more specifically, of the Roman Empire. He introduces the crucial concept of *horme*, that is, of an innate desire that prompts the soul to return to God. The soul, however, requires proper education through examples and doctrine; otherwise it can become misdirected toward worldly aims and society torn apart by its destructive power. Through the *Convivio* Dante felt able to explain the chaos into which Italy had been plunged, and it moved him, in hopes of remedying these conditions, to take up the epic task of *The Divine Comedy*. During this time Dante also began work on the unfinished *De vulgari eloquentia* (*c.* 1304–07; *Concerning Vernacular Eloquence*), a companion piece to the *Convivio*; written in Latin, it is primarily a practical treatise in the art of poetry based upon an elevated poetic language and is one of the first great Renaissance defenses of vernacular Italian. *De monarchia* (*c.* 1313; *On Monarchy*), one of Dante's greatest polemical treatises, expands the political arguments of the *Convivio*.

The Divine Comedy

Dante's years of exile were years of difficult peregrinations from one place to another. Throughout his exile he nevertheless was sustained by work on his great poem. *The Divine Comedy* was possibly begun prior to 1308 and completed just before his death in 1321, but the exact dates are uncertain.

The Divine Comedy consists of 100 cantos, which are grouped together into three sections, or canticles, *Inferno*, *Purgatorio*, and *Paradiso*. There are 33 cantos in each canticle and one additional canto, contained in the *Inferno*, which serves as an introduction to the entire poem. For the most part the cantos range from about 136 to about 151 lines. The poem's rhyme scheme is the terza rima (*aba*, *bcb*, *cdc*, etc.).

The poem's plot can be summarized as follows: a man, generally assumed to be Dante himself, is miraculously enabled to undertake a journey that leads him to visit the souls in Hell, Purgatory, and Paradise. He has two guides: Virgil, who leads him through the *Inferno* and *Purgatorio*, and Beatrice, who introduces him to *Paradiso*. Through these fictional encounters taking place from Good Friday evening in 1300 through Easter Sunday and slightly beyond, Dante learns of the exile that is awaiting him (which had, of course, already occurred at the time of the writing). The exile of an individual becomes a microcosm of the problems of a country, and it also becomes representative of the Fall of Man.

The Divine Comedy is a profoundly Christian vision of human temporal and eternal destiny. By writing it in Italian rather than Latin, Dante almost singlehandedly made Italian a literary language. By the year 1400 no fewer than 12 commentaries devoted to detailed expositions of its meaning had appeared. Giovanni Boccaccio wrote a life of the poet and then in 1373–74 delivered the first public lectures on *The Divine Comedy*, making Dante the first of the moderns whose work found its place with the ancient classics in a university course. Dante became known as the *divino poeta*, and in an edition of his great poem published in Venice in 1555 the adjective was applied to the poem's title; thus, the simple *Commedia* became *La divina commedia*, or *The Divine Comedy*.

In his final years Dante was received honorably in many noble houses in the north of Italy, most notably by Guido Novello da Polenta, the nephew of the remarkable Francesca, in Ravenna. There, at his death, Dante was given an honorable burial attended by the leading men of letters of the time, and the funeral oration was delivered by Guido himself.

PETRARCH

(b. July 20, 1304, Arezzo, Tuscany [Italy]—d. July 18/19, 1374, Arquà, near Padua, Carrara)

Petrarch, an Italian poet and humanist, was regarded as the greatest scholar of his age. His poems addressed to Laura, an idealized beloved, contributed to the Renaissance flowering of lyric poetry, and his consciousness of the Classical past as a source of literary and philosophical meaning for the present was of great importance in paving the way for the Renaissance.

Petrarch, whose Italian name was Francesco Petrarca, undertook his first studies at Carpentras, France, and at his father's insistence he was sent to study law at Montpellier, France (1316). From there he returned to Italy with his younger brother Gherardo to continue these studies at Bologna (1320). After his father's death, in 1326, Petrarch took minor ecclesiastical orders at Avignon and entered the household of the influential cardinal Giovanni Colonna.

Petrarch had during his early youth a deep religious faith and love of virtue. There now followed the reaction—a period of dissipation—which also coincided with the beginning of his famous chaste love for a woman known now only as Laura. Petrarch himself kept silent about everything concerning her civil status. He first saw her in the Church of St. Clare at Avignon on April 6, 1327, and loved her, although she was outside his reach, almost until his death. From this love there springs the work for which he is most celebrated, the Italian poems (*Rime*), which he affected to despise as mere trifles in the vulgar tongue but which he collected and revised throughout his life.

During the 1330s, which were years of ambition, unremitting study, and travel, Petrarch's reputation as a scholar spread. He was crowned as poet on the Capitoline Hill on April 8, 1341, afterward placing his laurel wreath on the tomb of the Apostle in St. Peter's Basilica, a symbolic gesture linking the Classical tradition with the Christian message.

He subsequently became enthusiastic for the efforts of Cola di Rienzo to revive the Roman republic and restore popular government in Rome—a sympathy that divided him still more sharply from the Avignon court and in 1346 even led to the loss of Cardinal Colonna's friendship. The Plague of 1348, known as the Black Death, saw many friends fall victim, including Laura, who died on April 6, the anniversary of Petrarch's first seeing her. Finally, in the jubilee year of 1350 he made a pilgrimage to Rome and later assigned to this year his renunciation of sensual pleasures. The time in between these landmark events was filled with diplomatic missions, study, and immense literary activity.

In 1351 he began work on a new plan for the *Rime*, which he had begun writing two decades earlier. The project was divided into two parts: the *Rime in vita di Laura* ("Poems During Laura's Life") and the *Rime in morte di Laura* ("Poems After Laura's Death"), which he now selected and arranged to illustrate the story of his own spiritual growth. The theme of his *Canzoniere* (as the poems are usually known) therefore goes beyond the apparent subject matter, his love for Laura. He also continued work on the *Epistolae metricae* (66 "letters" in Latin hexameter verses), begun in 1350; he embarked on a polemic against the conservative enemies of his new conception of education, which rejected the prevailing Aristotelianism of the schools and restored the spiritual worth of Classical writers. He also began work on his poem *Trionfi*, a generalized version of the story of the human soul in its progress from earthly passion toward fulfillment in God.

After a number of moves and intense work on the definitive versions of his various writings, Petrarch found himself in Padua in 1367. He remained there until his death, dividing his time from 1370 between Padua and Arquà, in the neighboring Euganean hills, where he had a little house. There he wrote the defense of his humanism, *De sui ipsius et multorum ignorantia*. He was still in great demand as a diplomat. Despite suffering a stroke in 1370, he did not stop working; in addition to revisions, he composed more minor works and added new sections to his *Posteritati*, an autobiographical letter to posterity that was to have formed the conclusion to his *Seniles*; he also composed the final sections of the *Trionfi*. Petrarch died while working in his study at Arquà and was found the next morning, his head resting on a manuscript of Virgil.

GEOFFREY CHAUCER

(b. *c.* 1342/43, London?, Eng.—d. Oct. 25, 1400, London)

The Canterbury Tales by Geoffrey Chaucer, the outstanding English poet before Shakespeare, ranks as one of the greatest poetic works in English. Chaucer also contributed importantly in the second half of the 14th century to the management of public affairs as courtier, diplomat, and civil servant. But it is his avocation—the writing of poetry—for which he is remembered.

EARLY YEARS

Chaucer first appears in the records in 1357, as a member of the household of Elizabeth, countess of Ulster, wife of Lionel, third son of Edward III. By 1359 Chaucer was a member of Edward III's army in France and was captured during the unsuccessful siege of Reims, and by 1366 Chaucer had married. Chaucer's career was prospering at this time. His first important poem, *Book of the Duchess*, is among the records that provide evidence of his connection with people in high places. That poem of more than 1,300 lines, probably written in late 1369 or early 1370, is an elegy for Blanche, duchess of Lancaster, John of Gaunt's first wife, who died of plague in September 1369. Chaucer's close relationship with John, which continued through most of his life, may have commenced as early as Christmas 1357 when they, both about the same age, were present at the countess of Ulster's residence in Yorkshire.

For this first of his important poems, Chaucer used the dream-vision form, a genre made popular by the highly influential 13th-century French poem of courtly love, the *Roman de la rose*. Chaucer translated that poem, at least in part, probably as one of his first literary efforts, and he borrowed from it throughout his poetic career. The

Duchess is also indebted to contemporary French poetry and to Ovid, Chaucer's favorite Roman poet. Nothing in these borrowings, however, will account for his originality in combining dream-vision with elegy and eulogy of Blanche with consolation for John.

During the 1370s, Chaucer was at various times on diplomatic missions in Flanders, France, and Italy. His career as a diplomat and civil servant was flourishing. So much responsibility and activity in public matters appears to have left Chaucer little time for writing during this decade. The great literary event for him was that, during his missions to Italy, he encountered the work of Dante, Petrarch, and Boccaccio, which was later to have profound influence upon his own writing. Chaucer's most important work of the 1370s was *Hous of Fame*, a poem of more than 2,000 lines, also in dream-vision form. In some ways it is a failure—it is unfinished, its theme is unclear, and the diversity of its parts seems to overshadow any unity of purpose—but it gives considerable evidence of Chaucer's advancing skill as a poet. In addition to its comic aspects, the poem seems to convey a serious note: like all earthly things, fame is transitory and capricious.

The Middle Years

Political events of the 1380s, from the Peasants' Revolt of 1381 through the Merciless Parliament of 1388, combined with his wife's apparent death in 1387, must have kept Chaucer steadily anxious. Yet he produced a sizable body of writings during this decade, some of very high order. *The Parlement of Foules*, a playfully humorous poem of 699 lines, is a dream-vision for St. Valentine's Day, making use of the myth that each year on that day the birds gathered before the goddess Nature to choose their mates. Chaucer also translated the *Consolation of Philosophy*, written by the Roman philosopher Boethius (early 6th century), one of the most influential of medieval books. Its discussion of free will, God's foreknowledge, destiny, fortune, and true and false happiness had a deep and lasting effect upon Chaucer's thought and art. In his next poem, *Troilus and Criseyde*, the influence of Boethius's book is pervasive. Chaucer took the basic plot for this 8,239-line poem from Boccaccio's *Filostrato*. Some critics consider *Troilus and Criseyde* Chaucer's finest work, greater even than the far more widely read *Canterbury Tales*. But the two works are so different that comparative evaluation seems fruitless. Against the background of the legendary Trojan War, the love story of Troilus, son of the Trojan king Priam, and Criseyde, widowed daughter of the deserter priest Calkas, is recounted. The poem moves in leisurely fashion, with introspection and psychological insight dominating many sections.

Also in the 1380s, Chaucer produced his fourth and final dream-vision poem, *The Legend of Good Women*. Perhaps the most important fact about the *Legend* is that it shows Chaucer structuring a long poem as a collection of stories within a framework. Seemingly the static nature of the framing device for the *Legend* and the repetitive aspect of the series of stories with a single theme led him to give up this attempt as a poor job.

Last Years and *The Canterbury Tales*

Chaucer's great literary accomplishment of the 1390s was *The Canterbury Tales*. In it a group of about 30 pilgrims gather at the Tabard Inn in Southwark, across the Thames from London, and agree to engage in a storytelling contest as they travel on horseback to the shrine of Thomas à Becket in Canterbury, Kent, and back. Harry Bailly, host of the Tabard, serves as master of ceremonies for the contest.

The pilgrims are introduced by vivid brief sketches in the General Prologue. Interspersed between the 24 tales told by the pilgrims are short dramatic scenes presenting lively exchanges, called links and usually involving the host and one or more of the pilgrims. Chaucer's death, in 1400, prevented him from completing the full plan for his book; the return journey from Canterbury is not included, and some of the pilgrims do not tell stories. Further, the surviving manuscripts leave room for doubt at some points as to Chaucer's intent for arranging the material. The work is nevertheless sufficiently complete to be considered a unified book rather than a collection of unfinished fragments.

Use of a pilgrimage as a framing device for the collection of stories enabled Chaucer to bring together people from many walks of life, and the storytelling contest allowed presentation of a highly varied collection of literary genres. Because of this structure, the sketches, the links, and the tales all fuse as complex presentations of the pilgrims, while at the same time the tales present remarkable examples of short stories in verse, plus two expositions in prose. Over the expanse of this intricate dramatic narrative, he presides as Chaucer the poet, Chaucer the civil servant, and Chaucer the pilgrim; somewhat slow-witted in his pose and always intrigued by human frailty but always questioning the complexity of the human condition and always seeing both the humor and the tragedy in that condition. At the end, in the Retractation with which *The Canterbury Tales* closes, Chaucer as poet and pilgrim states his conclusion that the concern for this world fades into insignificance before the prospect for the next. In view of the admonitions in The Parson's Tale, he asks forgiveness for his writings that concern "worldly vanities" and remembrance for his translation of the *Consolation* and his other works of morality and religious devotion. On that note he ends his finest work and his career as poet.

LUÍS DE CAMÕES

(b. *c.* 1524/25, Lisbon, Port.—d. June 10, 1580, Lisbon)

Luís de Camões is Portugal's great national poet. He is the author of the epic poem *Os Lusíadas* (1572; *The Lusiads*), which describes Vasco da Gama's discovery of the sea route to India.

Camões was born in Lisbon when Portuguese expansion in the East was at its peak. He was a member of the impoverished old aristocracy but well-related to the grandees of Portugal and Spain. A tradition that Camões studied at the University of Coimbra or that he followed any regular studies, for that matter, remains unproved. He may have spent 17 years in India, but his time there has not been documented. He returned to Portugal in 1570, and his *Os Lusíadas* was published in Lisbon in early 1572. In July of that year he was granted a royal pension, probably in recompense for both his service in India and his having written *Os Lusíadas*.

The title of Camões's epic poem is taken from the word *Lusiads*, which means "Portuguese" and is in turn derived from the ancient Roman name for Portugal, Lusitania. The work extols the glorious deeds of the Portuguese and their victories over the enemies of Christianity, victories not only over their fellowman but also over the forces of nature as motivated by the inimical gods of classical mythology. The courage and enterprise of Portuguese explorers had inspired the idea of a national epic during the 15th century, but it was left to Camões in the 16th century to put it into execution.

It is impossible to say for certain when he decided to do so or when he actually began to write his epic. The 10 cantos of the poem are in ottava rima and amount to 1,102 stanzas in all. After an introduction, an invocation, and a dedication to King Sebastian, the action, on both the historical and the mythological levels, begins. Da Gama's ships are already under way in the Indian Ocean, sailing up the coast of East Africa, and the Olympian gods gather to discuss the fate of the expedition (which is favored by Venus and attacked by Bacchus). The voyagers spend several days in Melinde on the east coast of Africa, and at the king's request Vasco da Gama relates the entire history of Portugal from its origins to the inception of their great voyage (Cantos III, IV, and V). These cantos contain some of the most beautiful passages in the poem: the murder of Inês de Castro, who becomes a symbol of death for the sake of love; the battle of Aljubarrota; the vision of King Manuel I; the description of St. Elmo's fire and the waterspout; and the story of Adamastor, the giant of classical parentage who, at the Cape of Good Hope, tells da Gama he will lie in wait to destroy the fleets coming back from India.

When the passengers re-embark, the poet takes advantage of leisure hours on board to narrate the story of the Doze de Inglaterra (Canto VI, 43–69). In the meantime, Bacchus, ever ready to impede the progress of the Portuguese in the East, convokes a council of the sea gods and incites them to arrange the shipwreck of the Portuguese fleet. This is prevented by Venus (Canto VI, 85–91), and Vasco da Gama is able to reach Calicut (Kozhikode, now in Kerala state, southwestern India), the end of his voyage. There his brother, Paulo da Gama, receives the king's representative on board and explains the significance of the characters depicted on the banners that adorn the captain's ship (Cantos VII and VIII). On their homeward voyage the mariners chance upon the island that Venus has created for them, and the nymphs reward them for their labors. One of the nymphs sings of the future deeds of the Portuguese (Cantos IX and X), and the entertainment ends with a description of the universe given by Thetis and Vasco da Gama, after which the sailors embark once more and the nymphs accompany them on their homeward journey.

In *Os Lusíadas* Camões achieved an exquisite harmony between classical learning and practical experience, delicate perception and superb artistic skill, expressing through them the gravity of thought and the finest human emotions. The epic was his eulogy of the "dangerous life" (*vida perigosa*) and was a stern warning to the Christian monarchs, who, idling their time away in petty struggles, were failing to unite against the encroaching conquests of Islam in southeastern Europe. Realistic descriptions in the poem of sensual encounters, battles, and storms and other natural phenomena transcend the thrust of classical allusions that permeate the work and make for the high-flown yet fluent style of the poem. *Os Lusíadas* reveals an astonishing command of language and variety of styles and provides a fascinating portrait of an extraordinary man and poet.

Camões also wrote dramatic and lyric poetry. In his dramatic works he tried to combine national and classical tendencies, while his sonnets, elegies, and many other poems, all published posthumously, show the poet's full powers. As a result, particularly of his epic and lyric poetry, Camões had a permanent and unparalleled impact on Portuguese and Brazilian literature alike.

MICHEL DE MONTAIGNE

(b. Feb. 28, 1533, Château de Montaigne, near Bordeaux, France—d. Sept. 23, 1592, Château de Montaigne)

In his *Essais* (*Essays*) the French writer Michel de Montaigne established a new literary form—the essay—that he used to create one of the most captivating and intimate self-portraits ever given.

As a young child Montaigne was tutored at home according to his father's ideas of pedagogy, which included the exclusive use of Latin, still the international language of educated people. As a result the boy did not learn French until he was six years old. He continued his education at the College of Guyenne and eventually at the University of Toulouse, where he studied law. He entered into the magistrature, eventually becoming a member of the Parliament of Bordeaux, one of the eight regional parliaments that constituted the French Parliament, the highest national court of justice. There, at the age of 24, he made the acquaintance of Étienne de la Boétie, a meeting that was one of the most significant events in Montaigne's life. An extraordinary friendship, based on a profound intellectual and emotional closeness and reciprocity, sprang up between Montaigne and the slightly older La Boétie, an already distinguished civil servant, humanist scholar, and writer. When La Boétie died, he left a void in Montaigne's life that no other being was ever able to fill. It is likely that Montaigne started on his writing career, six years after La Boétie's death, in order to fill the emptiness left by the loss of the irretrievable friend.

In 1570 Montaigne sold his seat in the Bordeaux Parliament and retired in 1571 to the castle of Montaigne in order to devote his time to reading, meditating, and writing. His library, installed in the castle's tower, became his refuge. It was in this round room, lined with a thousand books and decorated with Greek and Latin inscriptions, that Montaigne set out to put on paper his *essais*, that is, the probings and testings of his mind. He spent the years from 1571 to 1580 composing the first two books of the *Essays*, which comprise respectively 57 and 37 chapters of greatly varying lengths; they were published in Bordeaux in 1580.

Montaigne then set out to travel, and in the course

The French writer Michel de Montaigne created a new literary form when he began writing his essays in 1571.

of 15 months he visited areas of France, Germany, Switzerland, Austria, and Italy. Upon his return he assumed the position of mayor of Bordeaux at the request of King Henry III and held it for two terms, until July 1585. During his second term Montaigne played a crucial role in preserving the equilibrium between the Catholic majority and the important Protestant League representation in Bordeaux. Toward the end of this term the plague broke out in Bordeaux, soon raging out of control and killing one-third of the population.

Montaigne resumed his literary work by embarking on the third book of the *Essays*. After having been interrupted again—by a renewed outbreak of the plague that forced Montaigne and his family to seek refuge elsewhere, by military activity close to his estate, and by diplomatic duties, when Catherine de Médicis appealed to his abilities as a negotiator to mediate between herself and Henry of Navarre (a mission that turned out to be unsuccessful)—Montaigne was able to finish the work in 1587. The year 1588 was marked by both political and literary events. During a trip to Paris Montaigne was twice arrested and briefly imprisoned by members of the Protestant League because of his loyalty to Henry III. During the same trip he supervised the publication of the fifth edition of the *Essays*. He spent the last years of his life at his château, continuing to read and to reflect and to work on the *Essays*, adding new passages, which signify not so much profound changes in his ideas as further explorations of his thought and experience.

Montaigne saw his age as one of dissimulation, corruption, violence, and hypocrisy, and he considered the human being to be a creature of weakness and failure. The skepticism he expresses throughout the *Essays* is reflected in the French title of his work, *Essais*, or "Attempts," which implies not a transmission of proven knowledge or of confident opinion but a project of trial and error, of tentative exploration. Neither a reference to an established genre (for Montaigne's book inaugurated the term *essay* for the short prose composition treating a given subject in a rather informal and personal manner) nor an indication of a necessary internal unity and structure within the work, the title indicates an intellectual attitude of questioning and of continuous assessment.

The *Essays* are the record of Montaigne's thoughts, presented not in artificially organized stages but as they occurred and reoccurred to him in different shapes throughout his thinking and writing activity. They are not the record of an intellectual evolution but of a continuous accretion, and he insists on the immediacy and the authenticity of their testimony. "As my mind roams, so does my style," he wrote. The multiple digressions, the wandering developments, and the savory, concrete vocabulary all denote that fidelity to the freshness and the immediacy of the living thought.

EDMUND SPENSER

(b. 1552/53, London, Eng.—d. Jan. 13, 1599, London)

Edmund Spenser was an English poet whose long allegorical poem *The Faerie Queene* is one of the greatest in the English language.

Little is known for certain about Spenser before he entered the University of Cambridge in 1569. His first important published work, *The Shepheardes Calender* (1579 or 1580), can be called the first work of the English literary Renaissance. Following the example of Virgil and of many later poets, Spenser began his career with a series of eclogues (literally "selections," usually short poems in the form of pastoral dialogues), in which various characters, in the guise of innocent and simple shepherds, converse about life and love in a variety of elegantly managed verse forms, formulating weighty—often satirical—opinions on questions of the day. Spenser's *Calender* consists of 12 eclogues, one named after each month of the year, and was well received in its day.

Spenser appears by 1580 to have been serving Robert Dudley, earl of Leicester and to have become a member of the literary circle led by Sir Philip Sidney, Leicester's nephew, to whom the *Calender* was dedicated and who praised it in his important critical work *The Defence of Poesie* (1595). In 1580 Spenser was also made secretary to the new lord deputy of Ireland, Arthur Lord Grey, who was a friend of the Sidney family. As Grey's secretary, Spenser accompanied him on risky military campaigns as well as on more routine journeys in Ireland. Spenser may have witnessed the Smerwick massacre (1580), and his poetry is haunted by nightmare characters who embody a wild lawlessness.

For four or five years, from roughly 1584, Spenser carried out the duties of a second important official position in Ireland, deputizing for a friend as clerk of the lords president (governors) of Munster, the southernmost Irish province. In 1588 or 1589 Spenser took over the 3,000-acre (1,200-hectare) plantation of Kilcolman, near Cork. By acquiring this estate, Spenser made his choice for the future—to rise into the privileged class of what was, to all intents, a colonial land of opportunity rather than to seek power and position on the more crowded ground of the homeland, where he had made his poetic reputation. It was under these conditions that Spenser completed his greatest poem, on which he had begun work by 1580.

In its present form, *The Faerie Queene* consists of six books and a fragment (known as the "Mutabilitie Cantos"). As a setting Spenser invented the land of Faerie and its queen, Gloriana. To express himself he invented what is now known as the Spenserian stanza: a nine-line stanza, the first eight of five stresses and the last of six, whose rhyme pattern is *ababbcbcc*.

What is most characteristic of Spenser in *The Faerie Queene* is his serious view of the capacity of the romance form to act as a paradigm of human experience: the moral life as quest, pilgrimage, aspiration; as eternal war with an enemy, still to be known; and as encounter, crisis, the moment of illumination—in short, as ethics, with the added dimensions of mystery, terror, love, and victory and with all the generous virtues exalted. In *The Faerie Queene* Spenser proves himself a master: picture, music, meter, story—all elements are at one with the deeper significance of his poem, providing a moral heraldry of colors, emblems, legends, folklore, and mythical allusion, all prompting deep, instinctive responses.

The first three books of *The Faerie Queene* were published in London in 1590, together with a dedication to Queen Elizabeth and commendatory sonnets to notables of the court. Spenser saw the book through the press, made a hurried visit to Ireland, and returned speedily to London—presumably in the hope of preferment, which he received in 1591, when Elizabeth gave Spenser a small pension for life.

Back in Ireland, Spenser pressed on with his writing, and in early 1595 he published *Amoretti* and *Epithalamion*, a sonnet sequence and a marriage ode celebrating his marriage. This group of poems is unique among Renaissance sonnet sequences in that it celebrates a successful love affair culminating in marriage. Books IV, V, and VI of *The Faerie Queene* appeared in 1596 and are strikingly more ambiguous and ironic than the first three books. This burst of publication was, however, the last of his lifetime. He was buried with ceremony in Westminster Abbey.

GLOSSARY

allegory: The use of fictional figures and actions to symbolize truths or generalizations about human existence.

anecdotal: Based on unscientific reports and observations; describes a scene that depicts a story.

chorus: Describes a group of actors who, in the ancient Greek tradition, respond to and comment on the main action of a play with song, dance, and recitation.

dramaturgy: Theater arts, or the act of writing plays.

dream-vision form: A style of narrative poetry in which the main character falls asleep and, in his or her dream, experiences events having representational, instructive, or moral significance.

epic poem: Long and highly stylized poetry that details the heroic achievements of the main protagonist.

heroic: A type of verse form in which, according to literary critics, poetry of a certain language and age should be written.

meter: The rhythmic arrangement of syllables in verse.

paean: Choral chant to a god.

panegyric: A formal, public compliment, often offered after the honoree's death.

picaresque: Describes a story that involves a rogue or adventurer surviving mainly by his or her wits in a treacherous society.

qaīdah: Classical Arabic ode.

For More Information

BOOKS

Morey, Allan. *Twelve Poets Who Changed the World*. Mankato, MN: 12-Story Library, 2020.

Mucci, Tim. *The Odyssey*. New York, NY: Sterling Children's Books, 2020.

Seymour, Mary. *Chaucer's Stories Simply Told.* Lake Ariel, PA: Hillside Education, 2022.

Wilson, Seán Michael, Murasaki Shikibu, and Inko. *Tale of Genji: The Manga Edition.* Clarendon, VT: Tuttle Publishing, 2022.

WEBSITES

Dante's Biography

exhibits.library.villanova.edu/dante-illustrated/dante-s-biography

View portraits of Dante and listen to an excerpt of his poetry in Italian.

Poems of Sappho

www.uh.edu/~cldue/texts/sappho.html

An English translation of ancient Greek poetry by Sappho is presented on this page.

Poetry Out Loud

www.poetryoutloud.org/poem/joy-of-my-life-full-oft-for-loving-you/

You can read a short poem by Edmund Spenser on this page.

Rūmī

www.rumi.org.uk/poetry/

Explore this online collection of Rūmī's poetry, organized by theme.

Index